Other titles in the UWAP Poetry series (established 2016)

Our Lady of the Fence Post by J. H. Crone
Border Security by Bruce Dawe
Melbourne Journal by Alan Loney
Star Struck by David McCooey
Dark Convicts by Judy Johnson
Rallying by Quinn Eades
Flute of Milk by Susan Fealy
A Personal History of Vision by Luke Fischer
Charlie Twirl by Alan Gould

Snake Like Charms

Amanda Joy

Amanda Joy is a poet and visual artist living in Fremantle, Western Australia. She has written two poetry chapbooks, *Orchid Poems* (Mulla Mulla Press) and *Not Enough to Fold* (Verve Bath Press, USA). Her poems have been included in journals and anthologies, including *The Best of Australian Poems, Regime,* and *Toronto Quarterly*. She is a selector for *Creatrix Haiku Journal*.

Amanda Joy
Snake Like Charms

Poetry

First published in 2017 by
UWA Publishing
Crawley, Western Australia 6009
www.uwap.uwa.edu.au

UWAP is an imprint of UWA Publishing
a division of The University of Western Australia

This book is copyright. Apart from any fair dealing
for the purpose of private study, research, criticism
or review, as permitted under the *Copyright Act 1968*,
no part may be reproduced by any process without
written permission.
Enquiries should be made to the publisher.

Copyright © Amanda Joy 2017
The moral right of the author has been asserted.

National Library of Australia
Cataloguing-in-Publication entry:
Joy, Amanda, author.
Snake like charms / Amanda Joy.
ISBN: 9781742589404 (paperback)
Australian poetry—21st Century.
Snakes—Australia—Poetry.

Designed by Becky Chilcott, Chil3
Typeset in Lyon Text by Lasertype
Printed by Lightning Source

For my parents, John and Sally, who gifted me a nomadic childhood in the Pilbara and Kimberley, and also for Tim and all the The Healy Road Tuart Lovers.

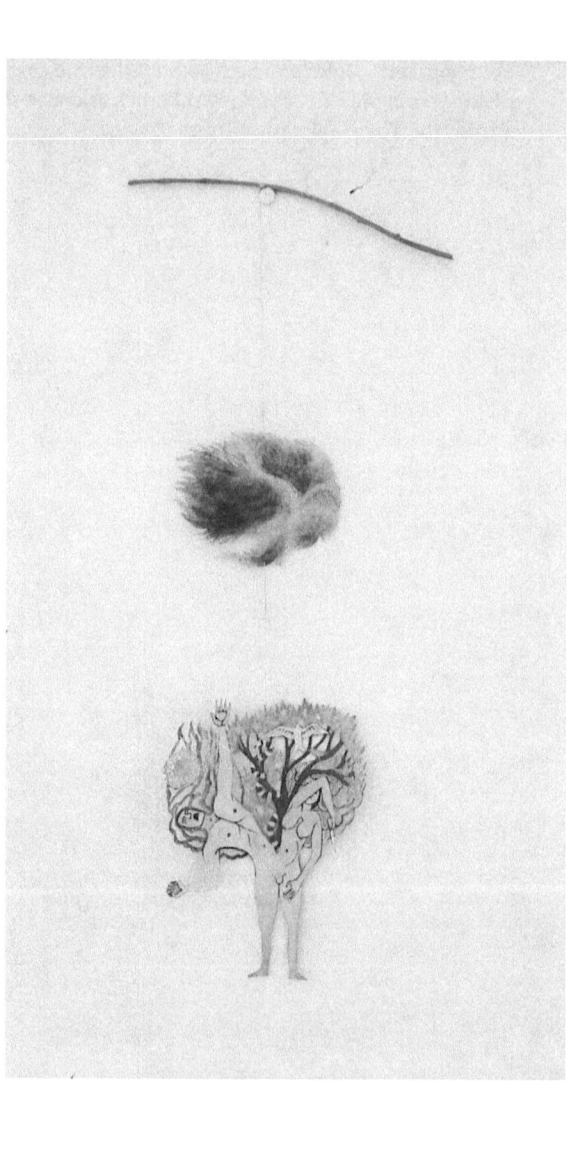

Be not like the sorcerers, for sorcerers carry their charms in boxes, but you carry charms and poison in your hearts.
Shepherd of Hermes

The grass of your eyes, bitter grass.
Eyelids of wax, over grass the winds pass.

The water of your eyes, forgiven water.
Paul Celan

… and the ants come out to the snake
and drink at his shallow eye.
Judith Wright

Contents

Part One

Almost Pause/Pareidolia **14**
Rhizanthella Gardner **16**
Nigredo **17**
Calligraphy **20**
Sud **21**
Wading Pool **22**
Carnon **24**
Tiger Snake, Walpole **25**
The Clutch **28**
Snake Skin, Roe Swamp **30**
Water Snakes **31**
Snake Eyes, Gosnells **32**
Cultivation **33**
Snake Woman **36**

Part Two

To Quell/ Riparian **38**
Gwardar Means Go The Long Way Round **40**
Spectacular Snakes **41**
A Python Near Broome **42**

On Warmth **43**
Tailings **44**
Medusa and The Taxonomic Vandal **46**
The Arrival **54**
Making a Meal of it **55**
Girt **56**
Chased Seas Urge **58**
Brumation, Waroona Dam **59**
Quetzacoatl **62**
Brown Snake, North Lake **63**
Rubedo **64**
Keeled Snake **65**
Sea Krait, Broome **67**
The Long Dry **69**

Part Three

Chambers **72**
Staying **74**
Matryoshka **76**
Solitude **78**
Etymology **79**

Part Four

Rise of the Phoenix **82**
An Athlete Wrestling with a Python **83**
Landscape with a Man Killed by a Snake **84**
Locus **85**
The Gigantomachy Pediment of the Old Temple of Athena Polias **86**
Poison Drawing **87**
Antidote Drawing **88**
Four Swans **89**
Atlas Moth **90**
Caduceus **91**
Tall Grass **92**
Drawn Resting **93**
Irma Bule **94**
Conjoined **95**
Synecdoche **96**
King Spider Orchid **97**
Sensed Through Opaque Windows **98**
The Tiger Snake Talisman **99**

Collateral **100**
Your Ground **101**
Vasilissa's Doll **103**
I Dream of Walpole then Drive to New Norcia Still Tired **104**
Blue Butcher Orchid **107**
Albedo **108**
Harmonic Points **109**
The Snake's Ghost **111**
Lost Dog **112**
It's 2013 **113**

Notes **115**
Acknowledgements **117**

Part One

*'Even the mother tongue admits of speech
only by turning us around'*
Ryoko Sekiguchi, Calque

Almost Pause/Pareidolia

Narcotics cannot still the tooth
that nibbles at the soul.
Emily Dickinson

Labile wonder, no rabbit-like fear, sea hares
filling the tide pools with their magenta ink are
flamenco dancers as much as mermaids were

dugongs. All those sailors mistaking the docile
monogamists for sirens. How often we graze
our hulls on rocks of clear vision. Still, we have

to see it with our own eyes, their turning tricks
their light desires, billowing in the space between
landforms, soft folds shape. Forest cockatoos

have entered the city. Baroque ripples in their
wingtips indicating stress. Married to what
we intuit as signatures, this persistent cleavage

A sickle shaped leaf at the base of one remnant tuart
slow chanted count of the mopoke above our heads
while in camp fire ash, the roughly laid out matrice

of squares on a turtle's back speaks of net. Here a man
quadriplegic has been taught by his mother to make
a sign of the cross with his tongue. Number

the things played out in the mouth. Language hesitates
to enter the concealed strand of vertebrae beneath
a dark lick of scales, uncoiling across blackened remains

of balga, racing as snake into our shared vision. Our
hands extensors and abductors gripping themselves
riven in resistance, the words 'beyond regeneration'

heard again in a stand of sheoaks. We can follow
the blood red trail of uneaten zamia nuts out
of scalded wetlands. Mining mountains no longer

unmoved, even this verse cannibalises itself
remembering the feast to come. Like, when I
use the word 'eternity', when what I mean to say, is 'water'.

Rhizanthella Gardner

*The sensuous signs offer us a new structure
of time, time rediscovered at the heart of lost
time itself, as an image of eternity*
Deleuze

Sequestered in earth, invisible flowering
truffled to fungus in wet dark. Sniff past
the ground, see past the crack in the soil
incise with fingertips the parted dirt to find
the threatened orchid, sessile and yawning
breath like honey

He rolls away from her and the smell of them
puffs from the sublayer of sheets, meeting places
of bodies wet and sticky shrink back in the quiet
away from the heat, sound sinks deep into
their inner ears

These hours are torn from their timeline, her heart
from its shape, her bare hands from their image
She is speaking inside herself and each word
burns long enough to clothe his back in what
she can't contain

Slow speed of night moving into the unseen
deadline of morning like a tongue into a mouth
stroking language

Nigredo

All sound comes
toward you
except the snake

scaled caesura
to your footsteps
their escape

Untangling
the grass in fast
strophe

Walking
for forty days
you come to love

their black ways
divining solitude
of warm earth

You crave sightings
Trespassing
plush mosses

to find scats left
blood-black and jewelled
with tiny bones

One wombed in
a holloway
of Devil's Pins

You lean in to see
its digestion
quickened by the sun

Two blue tongued lizards
in locked roll while you
stop for lunch

In slow rise
wind trips the saplings'
root-stirring gyre

You come to see all
light as a wake
and serpentine aubade

This impulse to name
everything only arrives
through absence

on the Cape
shoring waters recede
and land comes too

Waves rehearse
themselves endlessly
and slip under

The only witness
as a whale breaches
near the horizon

Lumped gullet
of migratory birds
all algae and insects

Behind you
a gentle snake is still
smoothing sod

A landlocked spring
welling in granite
Its depth a retinal black

Calligraphy

Watching you puzzling something
about on the back lawn, hunched
so far your head disappeared

A snake passed between us, lifting
its head slightly as you reached
for a lighter in your back pocket

I rapped on the window hard enough
for a crack to begin tracking a path
to the ceiling from its netted heart

When I looked back you were there
Your face overlaid in my reflection
both our mouths open at the stun

Sud

There were streets here. Calibrated now by disuse, once a road, this path is lined with Roman relics and an aqueduct leading to Pont du Gard. The air, crisp with Juniper, exposes my tongue to cold; distils the taste of my furry mouth; and I am held centre stage by the forest of my own movements. This is as close as we have come to silence, camouflaged by the stuttering of our feet getting away from us on a steep slope. You stop and the animal inside me is startled by your white teeth. You're pointing through the trees, there, at the edge of a water hole is Nina Cassian, on her knees, bent over the stag, tearing the dark flesh, chewing the gristle ear, bringing water to her lips. That hunger, washing through like heavy rain, unlocking smells, gathering sounds, is not mine. A pale gravity mingles with the disappearing sun. Only then do I realise we have walked too fast and I've missed things. My stomach growls to the food in your pack. Ahead is a clearing, wet with rot and a leak of light seeping into the black earth. It's too late now, to ascend to the next village, with its skinny cats, stone streets as wide as voices and shuttered windows. I touch your mouth, a canticle of tiny cobwebs stuck to my fingers, an edible dedication to the sticky underbelly of another past.

Wading Pool

The only one I killed
was in our garden
fear tripped and thrumming
blood deep in my ears
even after the threat
had earthed and gone
to ground

She had been still too long
Standing in the emptied wading pool
my daughter with the shortest temper
calmly motionless
all attention directed down

Through the kitchen window
I'd been watching her father
startling the steel strings
of his guitar
face obscured
by cusp of curtain
As he came in, I went out

Closer, my vision dipped
into the blue clam
all senses funneled to sight
Captive in plastic
meeting its own ends
a juvenile dugite
tracing swift shapes
between her feet
like a quicksilver jump rope

In a strange reel of actions
I clutched one tiny arm and swung
her over my head
high and too hard
Slammed her stunned wail
behind the screen door
then tramped back

Axe in hand
I pitched the snake to clipped grass
and before it could
thread through a fence
I'd jerked my arm full circle
and clouted between dark
of mask and olive length

Silence from the house
Lone in some grim trickery
Thrown open
the distance between
head and body
still writhing as though together

Carnon

in mid-Autumn is too new for ghosts
Eighties apartments steppe over the land into sea
A fretwork of empty jetties prattle water

Barely a soul here except your father
who can't sell his apartment until summer fills
the foreshore with bikinis and bars with champagne

We passed unstopping through Camargue to get here
I sulked as an oracular migraine bevelled
our mirrored outlines in the music-filled lift

He was already in the hall ready to take us
to the only restaurant open, had ordered meals ahead
His French made sluggish to his Sicilian tongue

and the stroke he hadn't noticed until we did
half his face stiff as this cold place and he blamed
dental work from two weeks prior

Collapsed, two visits and a box he wanted me to see
inside, Laguiole, bois de serpent, snake wood
Being bad luck to gift a knife, he kept it

Tiger Snake, Walpole

    We had left the path
in scrub, to watch dolphins curl
a wave, its lifting peak backlit
by a slanted glow of low sun
Dusk had settled, before
it dawned on us
        we wouldn't find it again

Wind-borne, level with our hearing
the swelling sea, its invisible history
of weather, deafening at its edge
gathered quietly in the backwash

A shadow between shoulders
of granite mimicked a track
and we followed it. Broken
ground fallen, unnoticed from
sight and feet, until the gap
widened as far down as across

Suspended on an open truss
of dead sedge, standing
a skeletal depth from earth
unstill as our half-held breath
You moved an index finger
to your lips and we listened

The sliding of an audible weight
smoothing a slower distance
Hissed a weft through dry grass
directly beneath us. Nornalup –
Home of the Black Snake

A sudden give in the delicate
joinery forced us onto all fours
Hands soothing the weave
of grey wrack, lifting
tension from our fingers

Warmth took a plunge with the sun
as far-flung sea spray encrusted us
Involuntary shivers splintered
kindling, snapping a release
of unseen wing beats

Every unprepared step gauging
the framework's brittle resistance
directed our blind movement upward

Water rats are waking up
they'll be stealing our food back
at camp. Eating our matches again

Offshore, the propeller of a vessel
White with science, sent to scry
glaciers, melting under the oracle
of breath, met with the inherited
skull-map of a loggerhead turtle
    left it etched to scale

Darkly hollow as sky before
moonrise. I don't think we spoke
Our innocent fear pairing us
with the snakes unseen below us
Their strange lungs pressed
always to the earth

The Clutch

Clumped in backyard grass
nine eggs, white as magic
mountaining the imagination
of a little boy

enough to be nested
in a box, inside a wardrobe, under
the warm stash of forgotten as
the mother snake returning
to find them gone
forgot them

Growth persists unwitnessed
absorbs what it can, leaving
the unseen crumple
of bloody shell

Seven hatch cramped
under the lid, behind the door
in the small boy's room, where
he sleeps each night

They silently trace invisible
shapes in the dark, near
shoes he hasn't learned
to tie the laces on

Looked back on in fragments
narrated with knowledge
the story

elision of threat
peril at the margin and like
a misunderstood sentence
two eggs, dull grey with rot
forever furled

Snake Skin, Roe Swamp

Shedding skin of a snake, will
loosen first at the lips, retract
backward over bluing eyes
dull crown, those sorcerous jaws

Resistance is needed, seeking
friction of rock, chafe of grass
scour and scrub of brown balga
it braces its body and slides out

Slipped fishnet of bubblewrap
mingled with a streaky mandala
of divested paperbark, becomes
my discovery, being its past

I tease open a brittle end, puzzle
my arm inside, until it is sheathed
to the elbow, ghost eyes puckering
my skin. My pulse, its unsealed centre

Vestiture of rain spittle in my hair
A cool trickle slides inside my collar
I tear the delicate mesh pulling it off
in what becomes a deluge

God of fragmentation, refusing
to keep things whole, coming
to me later. Showing again that
repetition might simply be
a lack of attention to detail

Water Snakes

... when bush people had the power
to sing to the snake.
Water everywhere –
Billy Marshall Stoneking

Your mobile phone has no reception here, not from miles back up the road, before the ten kilometre walk begins. People disappear here. Not missing, like in the city, where police can check their bank account and find activity. Here hikers notice a tent, canvas torn and flagging the rocks, a wallet open nearby, rifled through by quokkas. This landscape holds perilous stories, sucked away in helical swell and crush, Southern Ocean, a heavy rhythm broken by a freak wave and the emptiness it gathers before it lands. A friend caught his own near-miss on video, expletives, blood and all. You can read about portals in Forests of Arms no one comes back from, before you go in. I think I've always known when this land doesn't want me, put on my pack and traipsed back, goose-bumped and edgy. When he's in Perth, a Yawuru man tells the story of a night, out of fuel in country he shouldn't have been on, he set up for sleep in his trailer, came back from behind bushes to find, in bright corona of torchlight, a huge black snake striking the pillow he had been sleeping on. Striking and striking, he makes the shape with his arm and slaps a pointed hand into his palm. Sometimes there, it rains so hard the river escapes and is up to your knees before you can start the car, I told him. But it's this dry city that really scares me, I don't know where this tap water has come from. Its source hidden, taste metallic.

Snake Eyes, Gosnells

My father brought me snakes
and lizards, in the desert, gifted
wildness to the warm cave
of my palms, its wuthering
to my fingers

When a crane boom came down
and smashed his back, we moved
to town, that hungry animal sculpted
by its own bones, pushing outward
Came to learn the silent
violence in architecture

Cultivation

Distress. It comes like this —
A woman roiling words
outside the service station

Forest necropolis, ground
sprouting red marri saplings
two years after drought

false exult
of jettisoned seed
from the last branch
of a nesting tree

Weather becomes a template
when two degrees
signal cut outs and cuts
loose species.

Change is satellite, always
threatening to settle in
Water spooling backwards

unapparently gathered
and always partially obscured
these disappearing

snakes, harmless tails proffered
Show no country is stark when
marked by etching
of underbelly

Even I have woken
from dream meetings. Cool
tongue of body shaping my side
where it lay on earth

This week, stung by feral bees
my scalp burned and glands filled
maybe with dead bacteria
as toxins woke my blood's
violent defence

Sick enough to think sheep
in a paddock
looked like snow
I drove home
-ward to the nauseating rhythm
of electricity poles
scoring the sky

My son, asleep on the back seat
woke, to me explaining my speed
to police and asked to camp
before roos might start drinking
from the road

Coffee rock loosened
into conical mounds
Indecipherable and nascent
as upturned soil. Golden
thyrses of moodja stand
dramatic beside our tent, as

by torchlight we begin picking
more tiny ticks like black fruit
from our skin

Snake Woman
after Margaret Atwood

I became the snake woman
unable to hold terror long
Obsession became great enough
to enroll in a snake catching course

Disclaimer signed, silver crook
and hessian sack in hand
they closed a door behind me
Told me to hunt it out

Waiting for the after image of light
to die. In twinned mission we were still
I didn't need the odour or a quick
hiss of scales across

skirting, to be aware
it had been placed cold in a dark
lidded bin. Limply coiled
and venomous

No telepathy of scent, just
two live creatures in a room
not so much afraid
of the task ahead
more, the consideration

Part Two

They shall take up snakes
Mark 16:18

To Quell/ Riparian

When I took another man
into my bed, weeks passed
before I saw myself
trying to write your body
onto the page
            in absentia

I substituted a fold of wave
in graphite descript for the hollow
I'd found in your shoulder

Cross-hatched a gannet's sharp dive
and a swift delivery to the airport

the butcherbird's bloody beak
poked from beneath his balaclava

When I lay near you under sky
attenuated by needles of sheoak
we had slept and walked the river
            met at every mouth

I considered uprooting
the slow tracery of days clumped
at my legs. Misunderstanding
sacrifice   relearning it as seed
and three-valved fruit capsule

when you come home and all
the places you have been are left

to clotted light of recollection
beneath riparian trees, our finest
strokes always saved for
these finishing touches

More inclined to spread than grow tall
A sheoak's other name being kwel

Gwardar Means Go The Long Way Round

Coming across a group of boys laughing
while stoving in the carcass of a cow
with balga stalks, I changed my path

to a section of red riverbank splayed open
by weathering and animal tracks

Bent back to watch a kookaburra
watching me. I lost my footing and slid
with a barrage of rocks

in a confusion of vision and pain
kaleidoscopic flashes of what may have been
a gwardar, in panic knotting itself as
though attacked from all sides

Somehow I stopped
No sign left of any creature but myself
all torn clothes and shredded knees

In a conspiracy of senses, fragments
of snake have swallowed every other
memory of that day

Spectacular Snakes

Opening a book on Spectacular Snakes
    of Australia, on a friend's shelf, I flipped
from The Masters of Camouflage
    to the final chapter, titled simply
The Rest ⁓

I thought of you
    last night, saying, that's all anyone is
searching for ⁓

Rest. In a peculiar locution, moving off
    the tongue with the near-silence
of an unseen snake in the grass

A Python Near Broome

Watching the moon snake its glare
down a staircase of ocean, she turned
to me, foetal in a warm curl of sand
Thresholds of dark shifting around us

until we remembered crocodiles

Water will conceal at a distance, splay
light, only reveal detail as entered
Burnished surface eddying from your
hands, inky shoals beneath your thighs

Dizzy with wilderness, we pitched

camp without poles, strung canvas up
to a bloodwood tree, swept crystals
of resin and broken limbs from its base
If definition brings trust I remember

a python we found carpeting our tent

Patterned skin conjuring flecked light
length gnarled by a swallowed toad
I dragged it out by the tail and we slept
in its place, damp hair salting our pillows

Close to morning I could hear the slow

hiss of scales against nylon, see its shadow
ease away from where it spent the night
As near to me as her or the riffling wall
both flare and dark ruptures

On Warmth

(To Cross Out Each Sound With a Word)

... don't let any parts of us be amputated that could be expansive for us.
Irigaray

Coming back.
A map can be heard in a hive's song of wings,
to follow, with soft dark feet. I have positioned
my chair about two metres behind the others,
the legs pushed deep into the turf.

Your hair is longer, more grey, your lips thinner.
A less dramatic sideshow. I follow your breath by
the lift and drop of your shoulders, the finger
tracing the podium.

The sun throbs behind my lobes. I am too far for
your words, just outside their reach, I imagine
skeins, some transparent consonants, stretching
towards me,

divest of their meaning, I could touch them, just
the sensation of an S whistled through the abacus
of your teeth, resting on my fingertips. I spread
my hands upwards

on my knees to catch them, the mathematics of
your sound. Later in bed, when you ask me what
I thought, I touch your lips, lean forward to push
my tongue into your mouth.
Into the swarm.

Tailings

Call one thing another's name long enough, it will answer
Jane Hirshfield

Eyelets of cosmos, anaemic stars, only gazing in words. That parrot
bush called budjan with its supernova of stamens, spurious and sacral
Initiate of glinting conversation with long-beaked cockatoo and bee

Hunger is the dugite resigned to regurgitating a blue tongued lizard
Its shingle back unpierced as it swings away, reefing its legs past a dead
raven unsettled by maggots, used condoms, me taking a photo

A man searching the swamp for a hook-up on Grindr scans my hand
for a phone, his vulnerability touching as he passes soundlessly
Keens into the whiteness of paperbark trunks and anonymity

I've been walking, barely felt Prickly Moses exposing flecks of blood
to garnet on my arms in the heat, which kindles this wildness in me
I can't name and meet each time as a stranger, forfeited to sleep

My suitcase yawning at the foot of his bed, him spilling cunning lines
across
new sheets as the mirror trembles with a passing train. I know the shame
of wanting him to call me, before distrust stakes its claim on memory

There are worse things than fire. Thriving, a tingle tree, heartwood
burnt out
centuries ago, shelters a school tour from a deluge in its still-black bethel
One girl lingering, is moved on by a teacher yelling that she won't drown

How it all turns in and swallows, thinking in unison as everything is
knotted, from trees to throats. Swelling panicle of micro orchid trodden
down to mandibles of ants, their mass smothering a flinch of baby bird

Scudding dragonfly plucked from the wind by dazzle of bee-eater, knows
catastrophe. Congested telepathy of letters nesting on my desk, a ruin
of truth, part flight, breezing devotion through an open door

Here with my son, mantising gooseberries to our mouths in undergrowth
A thrall of silvereyes quicken the fig as a neighbour spits words at her dog
Galahs shear sunflowers above us. Before it rains, I'm burying the seeds

Medusa and The Taxonomic Vandal

All eyes cast glassy, even so
hers, less bestial yet turned
an unwept red

*

Lower than a snake's belly
were Medusa's sweet ears and they
betrayed her

Whelked helical of coral pink, deaf
to the threat as she slept, of Perseus
his petrified mirror

The snakes slept too, curled like cochlea
scales cool and smooth against her
scalp

*

A stiletto viper can leave
pain in a snagged hand for years

Keeled fangs yank back
and widen the wound to
absorb more venom

A man naming one Shireen
after his wife is labelled
a taxonomic vandal

Only she heard him
correctly when he said it was
a means of apology

*

All the way, water
held his weight and his name

Following the scent of prospect
Perseus, sacker of cities

*

New ruin, burnished wrack, keystone
of first words. Actractapsis –

the side stabbing snake can bite
with a closed mouth

*

She, wild with absences. He
blooded with longing

their tangled edges, open mouthed
and hissing under ledges

*

Involute, dead nerves beneath
teeth will abscess

Watch them to encase each
soft word as knowledge
Scars sinking beneath skin

As he studies the indent of grass
where an animal had slept
the night before

*

Burrowing shushed earth
a dropped tail of lizard
can block the path down

so the asp has developed to fold
back on itself and escape
the hole

*

Relict myth cradled too close to the
ear, crackling with the inexact
encircled like wisdom through
dithering smoke

*

Fastened in her eye, again
the borrowed story

Vertiginous quick dip
of limbic to prey

Every retelling, a shroud
Hessian weft stained with honey
burred on wire

*

The mirror is not there
in every telling but the reflection is
Diminished

*

Dazzled to stone
stoppable life

Black water fish shudder once to light
then darken into gone

A swell, slow as mourning breaks
into sandstone grit

*

Bored nomads built towns
from healing metals

To be bitten on the heel
is to stop walking

*

Amateur taxonomy splits
the internet with revision

First in, first reserved
Namer's place in history
tramped back

Golden blade, pinprick

*

Who hasn't felt rage rise
in the spine at not having
their eyes met

wondered how many heads
it might take to dissipate it?

*

Split tongues are shared
by hummingbirds and snakes
to sense prey or choose a mate

imitated in the body piercing shop
Carnate, mortal and named

Medusa in five styles on the wall
needled into collagen

*

She was pregnant with sea salt
and suddenly headless
eternally looking
at herself

and you want to focus
on what sprung from her head?

Rank taxa
Blood, foam and two
winged horses

The Arrival

An unanticipated arrival with a box of paintings from New Norcia, delivered inner city. It poured onto floor, quickening the patterned carpet, a fast shard of olive green light no one stopped to look long at. Room emptied and brightly silent, it took sanctuary in the dark triangle of an upturned chair, as outside the shut door, windows filled with faces, eyes shaded beneath cupped hands. The legal office for the day made terrarium.

Making a Meal of it

Flinty incision
The skinning knife, white as a wing
Gestures a bending length, cuffs
the stricken head to dirt

The snake become carcass, swan
neck, short rope. Innards fingered out
Flesh left pink as palms of hands
but softer and coated in spittle

Cauterised by indifferent light, meat still
moving in the enamel bowl. The cooking
fire hisses in spinifex as flies arrive
to blacken the table

Somewhere in the clumped guts
a heart with no fear left in it

Girt

'Oh, I wish I could have uttered the Syllable and the High Sound
 that could pierce the Fish's ear
 and startle the White Owl in her sleep.'
Nina Cassian

Short dormancy, the heatless tryst, tamed state
Dead startle of gun fired into the scattered flock, thud
of price where I hear lack of water, where I
will grieve for something to thrash against

Standing ground, in mutual freeze the Little Eagle
we came across in low scrub hooking brains of a rabbit
through scalped bone, half skull a bowl beside still warm
fur, how we envied the swiftness with bad conscience

From the sea, a scuttled coast spews birds from high cliffs
tall trees stir the sky the way nationalism makes of each
landscape a bestiary. Bluefin in mercurial school carry a void
moon over water, its planetary attachments displaced

Sleep talk adumbrates, that morning you woke first
and left me with sliced mangoes for breakfast, the geodesy
of precise knifing capsized beside our bed, emptied of its thick
seed, my own declension collective in limp sink of mattress

Gill slits of the beached fish stopped open and sky dried
The sea horses just disappeared and fairy penguins rotted
in contusions of blue weed and there's not enough anger
I'm keeping my lamp well-oiled for the coming firebrand

Ground of doubt, cracked as empty creek bed rewriting itself
netlike, as bull ants pace territory. When you wrote me far
away my skin dried out and felt like artifice, so I used it to
soften other men. In dull tracery desire was latent and sold

In unsolvable drought, life drags all dead things to the surface
with white teeth to be nosed by gaunt dogs. Unsound echo
from a gulf in the ocean floor meets a double vision of fossil light
Snared in the strobe, branches of black ink hide a Giant Squid

Frightened crabs tickle their way back to cracks in the granite
soon lined bright with claws coloured like the lava Nijinsky
dreamt ran through his veins, each beat a tiny earthquake
in the cilia of his ear would tsunami fire to his toes

Along the beach a crowd gathers around bronzed German
backpackers trying to usher a dugite back into waves
they thought it came from, shaking their Southern Cross
towels like matadors, laughter surrounding them

Entr'acte. Standing uneasy with shivering gulls gripping
the rails. Your arm holding me to the boat's kilter. Each
rippling crest increasing unnoticed until the sway
knocks the books down from the shelf

Chased Seas Urge

In the mangroves, we avoid the shade black with swarming sandflies. I know I should tell you. I should say, I know I would tell you. But the sun is going down and the tide is coming fast and invisible as fear. Swallowing the partings. The shadows are growing longer and we have to walk further into the water to avoid the bites that will itch for days. Your back is covered in black flies hitching a ride. I follow the wake left by your strong legs. I am strong too, but smaller, the sea has a hold on more of me so I try to use my cupped hands like paddles. I have that curiosity, what happens if I let go? Give way to the pull, go with the flow. I mean you hear stories. Behind the island is a whirlpool, the old man told me last night. He told it better than I remember it. You turn to smile and that knowing is closer than the shadows. My toes feel the sharp roots in the mud, more tiny cuts to keep clean. There is a deep waterhole, more an undersea landhole here, somewhere, we fished it yesterday until the turtles snapping the lines won, competition, not a battle and I cried to think of the hooks in their stomachs. Then you said 'sshh, there's enough salt water here'. The Bardi woman came with a spear and caught one real quick and we shared her family's meal. My mind is there now with the turtles and the fish we didn't eat. We need to hurry. Creature and creature relocate now, at dusk. Some will eat each other. Soon it will come down to a choice between the bites and currents that will sweep us out fast to sea. Discomfort will win.

Brumation, Waroona Dam

i

Unlike me, to kick over a dead balga
looking for bait, but it was
dusk and redfin were gently spiking
the underside of the dam
So I went to finger out bardi grubs
their bloated white clots burrowed
brightly in charred branches
Anger flashing up my spine

ii

We had fought the entire drive
Stereo broken and wind shrilling
a gap in the window

Hearing ourselves repeating ourselves
over and over in the unfriendliness
of a blurred landscape

iii

We stopped the car at a scree
brawl of rocks at the base of a slope
sharpening the edges

of an artillery of cockatoo cries
I slammed the door on your questions

iv

Here is where we drink from
Dark reservoir sunk between
calloused hills and broken fences

I stopped there in half-articulated
arrival, surrounded by unseen movement
in tryst with silence

v

One kick detonating the jellied heart
of wood and over my foot flashed a cold
runnel of olive light folding like water
over rutted earth

The dugite, as long as the width of road
less asleep than we were
bent its body against a low crag
to fall upwards then rested
a few metres away on a granite slab

vii

As you reached me
your face unknowable
in a halation of orange light
my breath still lost in its holding

I leaned into you with the tenderness
only fear can bring and you said
voice soft and feral
as silver acacia — You know
even snakes avoid letting their blood run cold

Quetzacoatl

Fossils of snakes almost never retain the skull
Bones grown for expansion stretch apart one last
time and go to ground, evade being bagged
numbered and lost again. But not nameless

Unlike the bird wing ensnared in amber, feathers
and hair, colour refracting ancient light for aeons
Hollows still filled with the last air it cut through
before yielding to yoke of tree gum and resin

Air devouring a history of stone because all sky
is old and eddying, too busy exhuming warmth
to take up house long in the lung or heart. It returns
to holding outstretched the wings of a harrier

When communicating with the dead was common
and where. Per fumum, through smoke, broken
bread has left crumbs like carrion. Landscape
gestures reading itself in braille-like ridges

My friend's story is everywhere. Body writhing
blindly at her feet, decapitated by her father
The head attempted one last hiss before spiraling –
ligaments feathered behind, down a dark shaft

Brown Snake, North Lake

Somewhere close, the part
secret of two naughty boys
in gumboots standing on small
tiger snakes' heads

> If you hadn't shouted
> Stop! my next step would
> have been on her

This one was huge, brown
almost three metres long, slick
umber body languid across the path

As my eyes measured the extent
from visible to obscured, her body
hooked back on itself, arcing
sharply to rise above a shrub

Head, still as stone, tongue
tickling air. A question raised
at my daughter's fleshy thigh
clamped hard around my waist.

My slackened state shot through
again. Frozen before another
mother, willing my burden to be

still. Then, a place behind my ribs
which might conduct a hush
But more, the wild impossibility
of stepping away

Rubedo

The pickled snakes with salt-white eyes
lined the shelf above the cereal boxes
I passed them sideways, serving coffee
to men in suits with coke-reddened nostrils
(I've culled my resentment for the city)

When the café was quiet I would climb
up to touch the glass where they did
the tiny scaled trellis of their undersides
and my skin would prickle with heat
Sway my whole body like an opiate

When he would close the doors and return
to being a Chinese herbalist I would perch
on the bench nose to the jars searching out
a wound, some last substantial cicatrix
Their deadpan jaws unsurprised by death

His anger at returning to find me locked
out of the office with Soft Cell's Non Stop
Erotic Cabaret stuck in screaming orgasm
on the stereo. Now I can't remember how
old I was but he was forty years more

The first night I stayed in his room in the back
He slipped a clove of garlic into me and placed
his glasses where they could watch us
from the bedside. Within the time it took
for his breath to work me over I could taste
                    it in my mouth

Keeled Snake

These scales
keeled
as if all
surface
is mostly
water

divining
a cleft
between
salt-bed
crystals

spilling
across this
hessian weft
of flattened
grass

I envy
its design
to be so
impossibly
close without
chafing

tonight
uncurling
your hand
with mine

particles
swanning
darkly
between us

Sea Krait, Broome

How slow an approach when viewed
from a distance. How more likely
the encounter if the ground is clear
A voice saying always 'go ahead'
    calls it freedom

Above the 27th parallel is the heat
I know as home, in my bones always
untouched by city's cool centrifuge
that refracts a kind of light
which bursts and vanishes on the spot

Heading North, I escape the fray
Green hem of the outskirts, roadside
façade of forest, hiding a casement
of burnt earth, silent as myself

Outside, a poet ghosts a window
Writing back into life his night
parrots. I drive lines from water
to water, guzzle roadhouse coffee

Warming up, there is a conflict
of appetite, a suburban tree, black
with cockatoos shucking almonds
A dolphin trapped in a rockpool

Cane toads storming the Kimberley
in wet, find it planted with sugar
An olive python curled under a van
belly beaded with feral kittens

After three days of seated travel
I lunge from the car, sprint the length
of jetty, deaf to the man screaming
warning. Only in mid-air do I look
down to the sea, the time it takes
to panic

Two yellow and black krait, vivid
bandwidth of danger, turning on
the turquoise surface, and all
I can do, is fall

The Long Dry

'Madness hath builded her house in the high places of the city'
Guy Debord

Men are hanging themselves unaccompanied
by sound in the dark hours before the bottle shop opens
Rope snaking a branch of pepper tree
at the lodging house

Empty tenement. Dark windows bruised by sky
lighting rookeries of collapse and fire crumbling out
until the whole street is vacant
and mud caked

In ragged brown of summer Verticordia I peed
near a midden of fleshy arils heaped at an anthill entrance
Watched them drag seed deep instilling
acacia in dirt

Withering of certainty spits hisses
The swamps filling with drillholes guarded by adders
Air churned with a fierce screaming
warra! Warra.

Dumbbell of yield and sequence
Through years of discipline I learned containment
or vice versa as natural as speechlike
Upward spiral of spell

A nested equivalence, this woundedness
Pinned fury petering in honeyeater as a Falcon plucks
its way to the warm core, feathers wafting
down to soft Eremophila

Sentences in the Bible begin with And God
As if starting was difficult and well populated
An excess of tangle and downcast
in need of names

The roof rats went quietly once
the python escaped to ceiling rafters of my father's house
its coagulation of coils echoing shapes
of a nearby bogong moth

Part Three

The Brookton Poems

for Talys

Chambers

In my grandmother's house
was a huge ginger cat, too fat
to walk, which no one admitted
ever feeding

Five months and still
not showing

I have to shuffle my feet
through the soft lolling bodies
to bang on the roof, stop.
I can feel blood and fur
drying on my ankles as
I get out of the tray to piss

In the graded paddock
there's nowhere to hide

I hear the returned focus as
behind me the torches catch
another set of eyes, sharp
cracks and ricochet fracture
the hard night

It's a cat, feral, screaming
now, sharpening
the air with pain
now and the boys
are laughing as I walk
back

Your face pale and
tight as the moon
I grab your gun

push past the boys elbowing
each other proudly and aim
at its head

As it slumps, the silence
releases us. You're smiling
at your Dad, who's jumping
around like a shot
rabbit – Jeez she can shoot
My lad knocked up
a good one.

For what it means ⁓
I grew up with guns

Staying

On her knees again
changing his dressings
My grandmother's
sunlit hands over
a wound that
never healed

*Five months and still
not showing*

Why I'm here –
This growing inside me
drawing me toward
the women and
their knowing

They're staying
home, watching
A Country Practice
leafing through old *Bride*
magazines
and it's not cliché
it's just what they do

I'm still going
out with the boys
in the utes, in my jeans
with their guns

and beer
It's what they do

I think of the soft bones
The ones that aren't
mine, hardening inside
my body, half-baked
bun in the oven

Your Mother is showing
me how to make cookies
for the men to take out
I want to be good
company

I want to know
about babies from women
who've had them

Which hidden parts
of us dilate, darken
or tear

Matryoshka

Always on
my grandmother's
bedroom wall, a picture
of a boy and a girl
climbing a tree
to a nest
and now

*Five months and still
not showing*

but, riding on the back
of a ute I'm feeling the weight
of the baby with every bump
hard on my bladder

An empty quiet
immense in the trees
circles us

The boys are shooting
rabbits, one backflips
into the air about a metre
and your father stands
in front of me grinning
His brown fingers slip quickly
into the limp body,
tiny but deep

They slide in and draw out
a glistening mass of pink
shapes, tied in a clump
Holds them out
toward me

The fresh, simple presence
of the dead mother
in his other hand

He laughs and says – I reckon
you'll give us this many
_good thing
not all at once eh?

Solitude

I woke them
coming home drunk
and disordered, years ago
How do you like your
favourite granddaughter
now? My mother said

*Five months and still
not showing*

Escaping a Bachelor
and Spinsters ball
Sick on one ladle of
fruit punch, I can just
make out a track
chromed by moonlight

What seemed to be
a metal pipe bent
itself up and toward
me light spilling away
from its rise

As I froze I felt a flutter
under my belt and envy
for the snake joining
shadows

The silence of night
its solitary escape

Etymology

Fairy tales were
what I read before
sleep in her house
from a huge book, left
near the bed

The more people I tell
the more I seem to show

We visit Wave Rock and
Mulka's Cave with its
handprints and story
of a cross-eyed birth
and devoured children

I want a word
for this place
in my stomach
behind where
tiny feet will press
beneath my ribs

some ganglia, twisted
spaghetti of nerves
apparently

You eat scones with
your parents, at the kiosk

Writhing with baby
frogs, tiny waterholes
pocket the rock

I scoop some out
Smell of dead ones
makes me retch,
alone, I get scared
walk back

Overlooked, the ants
Mulka was left to
once he was speared
to death

Words are words
We leave
with a T-shirt

Part Four

a prey for the image
Francois-Xavier Gleyzon

Rise of the Phoenix
after Paul Nash

Vermillion nimbus
           slung low over
earth silvered by neglected mineshafts

Here sprout bowers of blackened
           wood from dumb ore

Weightiness in hover as suspended
           with sulphured crest
the phoenix rears to mirror a snake
    rising from a black spiral

An Athlete Wrestling with a Python
after Lord Frederic Leighton

Inversed taxidermy
Stuffed from outside
cold stone with snake soul

Glistening scale
and licked skin returning
an animal musculature

pre-whitened hybrid
too hard to be taut
Over-brightly perfect

our gaze arrested
and carnivorous
all pinned grip and eternal coil

Landscape with a Man Killed by a Snake

after Nicolas Poussin

i

Running as if the corpse wasn't already green
as if the snake hadn't lain motionless in dark umber
this past four hundred years
Won't he look where he's going?
If fear brings a plague he will spread it from swamp
to every idyll of the landscape
the fishermen, the woman on her knees
in dirt, washing clothes

ii

Deeper shades invite disappearance, low green of forest, black back of the throat open with alarm, the lake's un-netted depths. This skin's pink has dissipated, a new puce in its place, coiled over with a freshly scaled light.

Locus

I was carelessly concealed
belly down on granite, fingers
untangling the slow creek
where it pooled and emptied out

when a shadow loosened itself
into an inky rivering of sheen
and black body

With no one to share the surprise
I closed my eyes and opened them
to find it, mouth to brown surface
swallowing silently, all thirst
and quench

Inexplicable how I wanted to be
that water, touched and soundless

Snake enters the pool, carries her
head above the river's identical
remake of its likeness. A double
helix of ripples streaming behind

The Gigantomachy Pediment of the Old Temple of Athena Polias

Another dead language, revived tongue first
into battle, head bowed, snake drooped
through each loop of aegis, the latent
flare of muscled effigy

(Exhume the awe, the lifting chorus
of breathlessness and dig the words in)

Eyes, empty as stone, lidded by stone
Unswayable, what's left of a foot stepped
warily in her path, leaving a world of giants
unguarded, black air towering above

Poison Drawing

Rorschach print of Rattlesnake Venom and Quink Ink
after Cornelia Parker

Caudal thought, some dark misadventure
leeched and blotched. Denial

a confrontation of folded paper
Identical impression, mottled softness

going on from its own centre
Paper's capillaries deckle

and feather. Black drawing
in venom elicit
other edges, interrupt

Disguised as ink
shade moving
through water

Antidote Drawing

Rorschach Drawing of Correction Fluid and Antivenom

after Cornelia Parker

Lick one, then the other, blanked layer
Blistered mistake amended

De formed like the start of a thaw
Laidlines visible beneath

each singular stipple
remedy in whited closeness

Little to show how
all was almost lost
What it is to be alive

Pegasus from Medusa's head
From a horse's blood
venom's harvest

Four Swans
after Peter Stafford

A black swan scissors out the white of its wings
another three crane, snake-like from the surface

of a new lake, atop plinths of their own reflection
For days it had been raining on the desert

leaving thin lips of water to bridge the landscape
And this is his painting above my writing desk

unceremoniously gifted to me on my birthday
Orange dirt thrown back at a lowering sun

Atlas Moth

Symmetry pointed
to an instant of limbic fear

Conjurer
dusted scaly on each lifted
wing, a cobra
twinned in strike

incorporated
queer provocation in red fur

here, even its cocoon
with a zipper stitched in
becomes
a coin purse

Caduceus

It is hard to trust a profession that cannot even get its symbols straight
David P Sulmasy

A printer's device
Trellis of solitude

For slant-eyed snakes
to poke their heads

Tall Grass

Memory kept alive in slow
dissolve of photograph, my father
half swallowed in wheat grass
holding the unknotted lasso
of a snake

Somehow, from the car he had seen
its tail ravelling into a holloway

My mother quietly reciting
no, Christ, John, no
over and over
from the front seat
camera hiding her face

On black and white t.v. I'd seen
a man with a knife cut and suck
venom from a woman's leg
I had a new pocket knife in my jeans
My brother did too

Our father, the Godly cowboy
calling us closer to the snake-
shaped dark lightning
bolt arcing from his hawked hand

Its protection different
All muscle, danger and grace

Drawn Resting

Charcoal rasps
vespers
as I try to draw
from memory

a beach near Ise
with soft rocks
that turn to powder
at touch

Gentle slippage
of ritual and
desecration

Irma Bule

Abrupt start
Irma, fangs half inserted
in her thigh is kneeling on stage
A slow bend of cobra semi
curls her body and disappears
between her legs
It could be a strange birth scene
Tinsel of blue skirt lifted over the head
of a handler bent beneath
prising open the jaws
and her music is stopped
as venom stokes its own flare
away from a drizzle of blood and she stands
sweating glitter through grease paint
The dreary cowl of snake is returned to a box
and Irma refuses antidote
gnawing her lips and the bored roll of her hips
slides the audience's eyes elsewhere
blue light is falling around the black moment
Her dance begins
a slow conjuring of death
emptying circles
Maybe she just wants to disappear
This far from her children
the abandonment of this dance
the only flight she is capable of

Conjoined

*Decay is not simply a middle term
between the grain and the ear of wheat*
Georges Bataille

Chinese New Year in a room
with little room, not enough
to dance, there are no chairs
nowhere to sit. A man telling
us he is a dragon

An algorithm with too many steps
becomes hard to follow, instructs –

Go down to the forest, with its absence
of human dimensions, until
you get there, Consider –

The spectral evidence
Having been seen on the other side
of town cursing a cow
while you were asleep
in your bed

The child afraid of the dark, given
a beautiful name impossible
to fill, sits in a doorway watching
two lines of traffic heading in two
opposite directions

The other child, papillionate
butterflied at the chest, cries out
vibrates on a page without pain
or colour

Synecdoche

Can't say —
poor snake
Your strangeness is maybe
what we can't imagine
living without

hands, ears, a good name
and company

King Spider Orchid

*'do you remember my house with the balconies on which
the light of June drowned flowers in your mouth'*
Pablo Neruda, from his poem 'I Explain Some Things'
(his poem to Lorca after his execution)

Slantwise, in the italic of quotation, another's thought
poised above my love poem to you, the grief felt by one
man at the death of another to politics' crippled blade
makes of his mouth a cave, a water-filled earth-womb

I could leave statecraft aside, forget the lit-up lives
of the poets, hold only the flowers clutched in their teeth
Alstroemeria no doubt, tubers and soil at their cheeks
and offer them to you like an orchid lip to the wasp-map

This recollection is handless and misses the fingerprints
of its thief, somewhere else stealing more ordinary things
a wet fogged bravery steaming out from forgetting, like
the window of your room that first estuarine morning

My voice is betraying Neruda, outside, his love for Lorca
beneath my balcony, his flowers an orchid, slow dark creep
of light flooding the heart with the legislature of distance
and affection, blood spot blossoms dividing man-poet

Neftali was his real name, he kept them both, at once like
my held breath at reading a soft line on my back, written
by your finger, same drowned light cooling crimson welts
Porous rock and soft weeds springing up at the foot of our bed

Sensed Through Opaque Windows

It's hard to understand architecture
when my past is sea and desert

It could be that these things are not
simultaneous

When you kiss me and the inside of your mouth is the colour of mulla mulla
it makes my feet burn. Then, I am standing on the red earth in the middle
of the day and a girl's voice shouts you look deadly sis
Beside you now in this rectangle of flowers, in the pocket of my black
jersey dress my fingers find forgotten cherry pits (I ate them to wash
those last words
out of my mouth)

These pieces of memories I haven't known
lie lightly

Undone by the closeness of the ocean, forgetting returns in pieces
With the skin of my body resting on the skin of your body
we form small patches of darkness between us –
as smoke, leaving the fire aspires to a more spacious form

Todays encased
in yesterdays
Tiny birds in eggshells

The Tiger Snake Talisman

Give me the snake bone
eyes in each vertebra
left when weight of flesh
has lifted

Garnet blood remembered and lost
to dark stone
Your signature is upon me says the talisman
recognise me and do as you will

I walk with you about my neck
More than emblem
a spine, so like mine
set to endure

Gateway of dark tunnel waiting
to call out a dormant echo
not banished but still

an uncertain distance
from my silence

Collateral

Crushed and baked into bitumen
Permanent marking an 's' it should
have slipped through a second or
two sooner, a black snake made blue

I had sat beside it in an hour of
thirsty heat, watching cars arrive
as globules from a vanishing point

Deciding to claim part of it, I eased
one finger under the tail and it lifted
as one rigid piece into my pack

Looking back to where it had been
I found no trace, no shadow, imprint
Hard tar, a finished business

Your Ground

                                    Its tongue
                            is the only thing moving
                              A striking distance
                                from your face
                              Sharp arc of snake
                            head flared with venom
                               A totemic weight
                               posted darkly in
                                suddenness of
                           grizzled air between you
                           Your body in mirrored freeze
                              still on your knees
                            swiveled from a lizard
                      you were attempting to capture
                             on a fistful of phone
                           Your jaws both clamped
                             over a rising silence
                           Wind is a litany of hiss
                         through grass and it arrives
                         at your eyeballs and the blink
                                brings release
                        snake melts toward the earth
                               its wilding light
                              shines and slides
                          A spilled surface of black
                               slick on the grit
                            The anthropologist
                          you were walking with
                         is bounding up behind you
                         and again the snake rears
                        yellow belly showing no fear
                         withers into twisting away

through underscrub
like an escape but slower
The luminous trance stays
for more than months
(you still can't remember
standing)
The psychologist says
your ego died (for
a few unsplit seconds)
Your friend, an elder
from Broome explains the snake
is your guardian
painting its likeness in repose
on bark you once fed a red
tailed cockatoo from
You hang it above
your writing desk
And for a while
it all makes sense
The brute matter
how dangerous you are
how safe
the circuitous journey
Then one morning you get it ⁓
That paired wisdom
your bodies made

Snake says
Be still
Stand your ground
It's the only protection
we have

Vasilissa's Doll

I am the house and the hut with chicken legs that turns to face us
I am the sea cave speared through by the foundations of skyscrapers
The glitter and shine of bare bones
the scaffolding and crane, tented buildings
outskirts of the forest with trees bent like ribs
Strange enough without shadows

Here I am, one hand in yours, the other searching for skeleton keys
in the soft cloth of her unwritten pocket. Private finger cave
of receipts, crumbs, stones and small change. Here is the dull-eyed doll
who comes to life at night, feeding my cheeks of milk and blood
as my hair grows down to my waist

I like to tell you this story, you, keeper of water and all
the paths it makes when trapped, bent forward in your chair
like the red rider, have asked me to close my eyes and feel
the quiver, Saraha haha
I laugh, I know you're winging it

This is grown in the dark too, in the chambers of involuntary muscle
and it will go one way or another. I am picking
the black grains from the wheat
When you tap me on the shoulder I turn
to nothing

I Dream of Walpole then Drive to New Norcia Still Tired

Bluntly sundered

Whale ribs along the beach

Not seen from a cliff as dropped eyelashes

Vision filmic as surface

Thought leaves nothing to scale

Language is its residue

Tremendum as the bug

Suddenly trapped under your eyelid

Fished out in bits

Stepping close to a curtain of wax

Of honey bees in a dead lion

Apices fixed where lungs began

Large stories are played out

Always in our small lives

Here / there are no false totems

We drove to the monastery

A pair of brown falcons sentinel

Their nest shaped to a chapel's crenulation

One window lit at twilight

Disused schoolroom painted with murals of muses

Soothsayer's familiarity with air

From a single thread of altar cloth

Science tracks history to

Dutch ships plundering platinum

Mined in Columbia

I search every painting for a snake

There are none

A lawyer in our party takes apart a telescope

The telescope is pointed at a wall

Between pink trunks of Powderbark Wandoo

The buildings are at a distance

A dead tree continues

Supporting life

Looking up for cries of Carnaby Cockatoos

We find them feeding on wild radish in low grass

Seemingly unthreatened

There's no animal alive

Won't meet your eye

We have missed vespers and the church is locked

Night drive home

Darkness bowls itself

Down the road toward us

Blue Butcher Orchid

Inking the fingers
dialect and echo
Blue Butcher of tongue
peeled from its industry
     from roof of mouth
to reluctant curls
turned slightly left, new
     implication in Orchis
sepal to petal
cupped calyx, funnelled
modified into a lip

Albedo

It was in her hand as she called
to say I should pick it up
The smell was unbearable
her eyes couldn't take it —
the feel of whatever
dead skin released
into air

She presented it to me across both
hands, as cerements or shroud

Found where they'd been given
move-on notice, between bee-eater
burrows and ancient banksia
obstructing a drilling rig

Webbed fretwork embossed by live
form, limned silver, light as my own
hair over my palms, it made a sound
against skin like summer grass

To me it exhaled pale silt
and swamp rushes, unearthed chert
a calenture, also

in lingering base
note as I brushed
it to my cheek, the bleached thread
my grandfather repaired
his last nets with.

Harmonic Points

One metre is one ten-millionth
of the distance from the Equator
to the North Pole through Paris
This is a useful measurement

Then there is the truth of ratios:
a bird's wingspan to a room
the opening in the window
it entered through, then lost
The weight of a pair of hands
trying to free it. There is the lonely
side of dialogue. The pieces
of the map and the ground
covered by your body when you fall
The cleverness you trail like
a comet. The circus and flea
Edson's ambushed stone to
the size of his mother's love. Some
giddy slippage, to all the harmonic
points on a line to infinity
The curved eyeball to the keyhole
of the hostage, then, the walls of
the captive. Lullaby of bedrock
to all it cradles. The hollow
of your hand to what I would fill
it with. The rose and what rose
There's writing on both sides
of the paper. Sensation
of speaking in tongues. All
those centred deities of blind voyeurs
to the spectrum of a single note

The other side of the river to
a fish. Totems and guttered stars
Death, ash, fire, warmth and smoke
A forced song of almost someone
in so many breaths, there is also this ⏝

Made flesh: what I take in
from what was said

The Snake's Ghost
after Rebecca Horn

On a full moon
bring the snake to water
with one hand
support its head
Elevate the tail
to the height
of your shoulder
be rewarded
as the trunks
of trees dance in mirrored
ripples of light
borrowed from the pool's
bright surface
touched by the two-
pronged tongue

Five times in as many weeks
I have been told
the story of a small girl
in India
fetching a saucer of milk
for an unseen pet
in her room
night after night
until finally the reveal
Her parents' eyes widening
as a King Cobra
unspooled its dark
from under a cupboard
Hunching itself low over
upturned hands

Lost Dog

Write firemarked. Their cries hackle
my hair, red tails breaking up with the sky
inscribe the blotched light with warning
I'm too heat glutted to heed

Trouble is burrowing, ground chinked
with roo bones, fibula broken by land
rabbit pocked and warrened. Two monitor
lizards thread each eye in the slope

A helicopter siphons a dark line
of lake, its animal noise scaring the dog
her collar breaking at the lunge
as she vanishes into charred underscrub

Between my boots in double bind
a black snake, underbelly all aflame, winces
and flickers an outline of lemniscates
Pours over my foot and off the path

As the wind swells, a white frond of smoke
plumes ahead of me, then another
and several more taper up all around
Their spacing a uniform distance
tracking the old ring road south

It's 2013

Handed a gold coin
a snake in four curves at its centre
and I am writing about snakes

The year of the snake
when my father was born
again when my son was born

facts belonging to someone
pocketed and held close

Notes

'Even the mother tongue admits of speech only by turning us around' is from Ryoko Sekiguchi's poem 'Calque' (P.O.L. 2001)

The epigram to 'Almost Pause/ Pareidolia', 'Narcotics cannot still the tooth that nibbles at the soul' is from the Emily Dickinson poem 'The World is not Conclusion' and the line in italics 'like when I use the word eternity when I mean to say water' comes from 'Leafless Orchid', Orchid Poems (Mulla Mulla Press, 2010)

'The sensuous signs offer us a new structure of time, time rediscovered at the heart of lost time itself, as an image of eternity' is from Deleuze on Proust, Gilles Deleuze (Continuum, 2008)

'Nina Cassian, on her knees, bent over the stag' refers to her poem in the anthology, *Staying Alive* (Bloodaxe Books, 2002)

'.. when bush people had the power
to sing to the snake.
    Water everywhere' is taken from Billy Marshall Stoneking's book *Singing The Snake* (Angus & Robertson, 1990)

'Snake Woman' is written to Margaret Atwood's poem 'Snake Woman'. *Interlunar* (Cape Poetry Paperbacks, 1984)

In the poem 'To Quell/ Riparian', the lines in italic 'More inclined to spread than grow tall' are taken from the book *The Trees That Were Nature's Gift* by Irene Cunningham (self-published, 1998)

'don't let any parts of us be amputated that could be expansive for us' is from *The Way of Love*, Luce Irigaray (Continuum, 2002)

'Call one thing another's name long enough, it will answer' is from Jane Hirshfield poem 'Salt Water Stiffens Cloth'. *Come, Thief* (Bloodaxe Books, 2011)

'Oh I wish I could have uttered the Syllable and the High Sound that could pierce the Fish's ear and startle the White Owl in her sleep' is from the poem 'It's a Pity' by Nina Cassian, *Continuum: Poems* (W. W. Norton & Company, Inc. 2008)

'Madness hath builded her house in the high places of the city' is from *Panegyric*, Guy Debord (Verso, 2004)

'a prey for the image' is from *Shakespeare's Spiral: Tracing the Snail in King Lear and Renaissance Painting*, Francois-Xavier Gleyzon (University of Chicago Press, 2010)

The poem 'Rise of the Phoenix' is written to the Paul Nash painting held in Art Gallery of Western Australia

'An Athlete Wrestling with a Python' is written to the sculpture of the same name by Lord Frederic Leighton, 1877

'Landscape with a Man Killed by a Snake' is written to the painting by Nicholas Poussin, 1648

'Four Swans' is written to the painting of *Four Swans* by Peter Stafford, 2015.

'It is hard to trust a profession that cannot even get its symbols straight' is from *A Balm for Gilead: Meditations on Spirituality and the Healing Arts*, David P Sulmasy (Georgetown University Press, 2006)

Irma Bule refers to Dangdut dancer Irma Bule who died on stage after being bitten by a cobra she was performing with.

'do you remember my house with the balconies on which the light of June drowned flowers in your mouth' is from Pablo Neruda poem 'I'm Explaining Some Things' (his poem to Lorca after his execution)

Acknowledgements

Of the poetry in this collection, 'Tailings' won the 2016 *Australian Book Review*, Peter Porter Poetry Prize.

'Almost Pause/ Pareidolia' was Highly Commended in the 2013 Blake Poetry Prize. The 'Long Dry' and 'Sea Krait, Broome' were published in Poetry Chicago, special edition of Australian poets (ed. Don Share, guest editor Robert Adamson), 2016. 'Snake Skin, Roe Swamp', published in the Fremantle Press Anthology of Western Australian Poetry (eds John Kinsella and Tracy Ryan), 2017 and 'Chased Seas Urge' appeared in The Best Australian Poems 2009. 'On Warmth' was published in ETC: A Review of General Semantics, 2009, Fort Worth Texas. 'To Quell/ Riparian' and 'King Spider Orchid' were included in the 2013 Poetry d'Amour anthology. 'Rhizanthella Gardner' first appeared in Orchid Poems, Mulla Mulla Press, 2013.

Poems have also appeared in *Regime, Australian Book Review, The Diamond and The Thief, Stylus Poetry Journal, Queensland Poetry Festival Anthology, The Disappearing, Red Room Company, Rabbit Poetry Journal* and *Cordite*

I would like to extend sincere gratitude to the editors of the above publications and to Robert Adamson for his calm and constant encouragement onward. Loving thanks go to Talys, Wylie and Cove, the poetry doulas; Coral Carter, Annamaria Weldon, Liana Joy Christensen, Jennifer Kornberger, Renee Pettit-Schipp, friends, poetic teachers and sharers; Nandi Chinna, Anthony Lawrence, David Johnson, Arnold Pudding Smith, Rose Van Son, Meryl Manoy, Tineke Van Der Eecken, Gary De Piazzi, Peter Jeffrey, Monica Elberink, Roeli Joosten, Nina Ferrari, Jurate Saisnatis, Claire Potter, Ryoko Sekiguchi, Goro Takano, Peter Stafford and with particular gratitude to Terri-ann White, for her powers of extraction, and the UWA Publishing team for their combined grace and patience.

Most importantly, I acknowledge with respect and gratitude, the traditional owners of country these poems were written in. Also to EARTH FIRST! and all wilderness defenders, custodians and those everywhere who inspire the protection of planet and people.

Snake says

Be still

Stand your ground

It's the only protection

we have

www.ingramcontent.com/pod-product-compliance
Lightning Source LLC
Chambersburg PA
CBHW020335170426
43200CB00006B/393